I0054251

TEN WAYS TO BE STRONGER AND HAPPIER

IT IS *About* YOU

PAULEE BOWIN

Copyright © 2020 by NOW SC Press

All rights reserved. No part of this publication may be reproduced, distributed, or transmitted in any form or by any means, including photocopying, recording, or other electronic or mechanical methods, without the prior written permission of the publisher, except in the case of brief quotations embodied in critical reviews and certain other noncommercial uses permitted by copyright law. For permission requests, write to the publisher, addressed "Attention: Permissions Coordinator," via the website below.

Publish@nowscpress.com
www.PublishWithNOW.com
@nowscpress

Ordering Information:

> Quantity sales. Special discounts are available on quantity purchases by corporations, associations, and others. For details, contact the publisher at the address above.

> Orders by U.S. trade bookstores and wholesalers. Please contact: NOW SC Press: Tel: (888) 5069-NOW or visit www.PublishWithNOW.com

Printed in the United States of America

First Printing, 2020

ISBN: 978-1-7341809-5-4

Mermaid sketches by Paulee Bowin

Dedication

To my mom and to Suki Kaur, as well as all the other strong women in my life who are now angels in heaven. Also, a big thank you to my dear friends who have encouraged me to keep trying and have provided me with constant inspiration. Much love to you always.

I want to extend an extra special thank you to my dear friends Elan Lantz and Maria Metropolis for sharing their friendship, loyalty, and unique perspectives to make the books successful.

Contents

PART ONE

Perseverance

CHAPTER ONE

Own Your Place
in the World

From the day we are born, each of us struggles to figure out where we fit in, where we are meant to be, and who we are meant to become. I've always identified with mermaids—even though they aren't real—because they are creatures that don't fit into either world: land or sea. For me, that journey to find my place was so much harder, partly because I found out when I was four that I wasn't who everyone told me I was. I think that had a major impact on both how I viewed myself and on other peoples' opinions of me.

I always felt different from everyone else. At some point, I realized I didn't look like everyone else in my family, so I started asking questions. I was precocious and curious by nature, and relentlessly bombarded my parents with questions until they finally admitted that they had adopted me when I was eleven days old. No matter how much my mom insisted that I had been wanted because she had asked for me and desperately wanted me when they adopted me, I couldn't shake that feeling of being rejected.

Did my birth mom give me away because I wasn't good enough somehow? Was she angry that she'd gotten pregnant with me? Glad to be rid of this human who had complicated her life? These questions plagued my life and were part of what undermined my **confidence**. But what hurt me even more was the way other women treated me. Their bullying fed the parts of me that didn't feel good enough or wanted.

BULLYING DOESN'T END IN HIGH SCHOOL

My parents were wonderful but, like many children, I was bullied and teased most of my childhood. I became fascinated with mermaids because they were these mythical creatures who were a mix of land and sea, both fascinating to and feared by anyone traveling across the ocean. My **imagination** helped me through some of the toughest times because I would get lost in the stories I read, and then I'd create stories of my own. I imagined becoming a mermaid, beautiful and free from all of the pain, and swimming all over the world to new places. I pretty much did anything to keep my mind occupied so I didn't think about the bullying. I memorized the names of all the actors in my favorite shows, the lineup of the Kansas City Royals, all fifty state capitals, etc. Memorization and reading became my **coping** mechanisms.

However, I still struggled. No matter how 'smart' I became or how pretty I was, it was never enough to gain acceptance. Even as early as second grade, I remember girls ganging up on each other and on me. I was repeatedly called ugly, different, weird, too small, and too sensitive. All that cruelty added to my feelings of being unwanted, useless…and for a long time I wondered why I was born at all. Even as an adult, I sometimes struggle and hear those words echo in my head.

This intense girl-on-girl conflict continued sporadically throughout elementary school and had a devastating effect on my self-esteem. I was so busy losing the battle of trying to gain their **approval** that I began to hate myself, and my perception of myself was permanently colored.

So many of us reach this point and suffer long-term and life-altering consequences as we grow into teens and women. Bullying is very real and very detrimental, and is something that should never be dismissed. As young girls, we don't realize how significant an impact those childhood wounds can have on us as adults. Even when we are grown up, we minimize the effects other people's words have on us.

Be Atagartis

The first mention of a mermaid in ancient literature is associated with Atargatis, the Syrian goddess of fertility. She was responsible for the protection and well-being of the people who worshipped her. Legend has it that she dove into the sea, but only the bottom half of her body transformed into a fish.

Bullying is so prevalent in this world, for children and adults. Become Atagartis for yourself and the people around you:

- Recognize the bullying is happening.
- Realize that bullying is about the other person's insecurities, not yours.
- Step in and say something; shining a light on a problem is the only way to bring it out of the darkness.

The girls who bullied me did so to the point where I would go home and puke, then beg my parents to move me to another school. There were days when I contemplated suicide because I just wanted it to end. Every time, I pulled myself together and reminded myself that I was unique and special just as I was, and I wasn't going to let those girls succeed in destroying me. It was a gradual process, but I learned to be okay with myself exactly as I was.

For most women, being okay with who we are right this second is a daily battle, partly because of those childhood wounds. We struggle to be perfect as mothers, partners, business people, students, daughters…everything. We stress over the soufflé and the floors and worry that we are too anxious or too crabby or too loud. We fuss in the mirror and count every calorie. It's an exhausting battle; and here's the ironic part—we are doing all of that stressing to fit into a world that already loves us.

Let me say that again, just for emphasis: **We are doing all of that stressing to fit into a world that already loves us.**

Have you ever seen the movie *Mean Girls*? The characters in that movie are experts at bullying but making it seem like they're being friendly. The backhanded compliments, the exclusion of other girls, the gossiping? All of these things happen every day in schools and workplaces around the world. Cyberbullying has become a huge problem, so much so that some school systems are launching educational campaigns to help kids understand the damage it can inflict, as well as combat the cruelty. *Mean Girls* is a comedy, but it does shine a light on how girls often treat each other, as well as how we treat ourselves when we get caught up in that kind of world.

As much as we are guilty of judging ourselves, many of us are also guilty of **comparing**. As a teenager, you look at the girls wearing name brands and those who aren't, or compare your Keds and Target shirts with another's designer labels. Doing that is so dangerous because it sets you up for failure—no matter how much you compare yourself with others, someone else will always have more. Comparing yourself to others steals your joy.

What happens as a result of this kind of judgement is self-loathing. The media only perpetuates this by glorifying people like the Kardashians and giving a lot of air time to tell us which brands are cool and which aren't. Advertising is designed to make you feel like you must have that purse or those shoes in order to live a happy life.

For most of my life, I have never felt good enough for relationships, happiness, or success. I've felt like I didn't measure up because I didn't match some societal "norm". I know I'm not the only woman who has struggled with that; so many of my friends say the same thing. Many people who battle with self-loathing or a sense of inferiority try to control or soothe those feelings with unhealthy choices like eating disorders, addictions, or abusive relationships. We feel like we deserve this unhealthy treatment instead of standing up for what we deserve.

Women who are not okay with themselves sometimes grow up to become bullies. For some people, tearing others down is the way an insecure person can lift themselves up. It creates a vicious circle of meanness, guilt, lower self-esteem…rinse and repeat.

Adult bullying isn't as easy to see. The name-calling, fighting, and games that kids play aren't as easy to spot in adults because the bullying is more subtle. Behaviors like disregard, arrogance, gossip, spreading lies, and small criticisms, all fall into the bullying category. Adult women can be even more malicious in their bullying, even if it's not as obvious as it is in middle school. Learning how to recognize subtle bullying is key. Is your stomach in knots, are you obsessing about dealings with other people, or are you feeling inferior? Bullying from other people may be the reason.

The first step in dealing with bullying is **awareness**. Recognize that what this person is doing or saying is triggering your insecurities—and then **detach**. Detaching is difficult because we get emotionally wrapped up in what is happening, but *detaching stops the impact of bullying in its tracks.*

Detaching means stepping back and looking at the moment or the other person as if you are an outsider. It means not taking what happened personally (which I know can be hard) but recognizing that the person who bullied you has some issues, and you're just not going to engage with him or her. If you have trouble doing this, try physically taking a step back from the person so you put physical and then mental space between yourself and their behavior.

Next, **validate** your own feelings in that moment. You are not crazy. Bullies know what they are doing. Remember, they have decades of experience and are quite adept at making you feel bad so they can feel better. Do not take ownership of or responsibility for their nasty behavior; because it is *not your fault*. Bullies are often insecure, broken individuals who enjoy hurting others.

When I stopped judging myself by the standards of others, and instead **embraced** who I really am—quirks and all—the world became a less threatening place. By nature, mermaids don't swim around afraid of what others think of them. They boldly and unapologetically express themselves and explore new territories. A mermaid would say: *If those around you don't appreciate you, swim on.* And that's what I choose to do.

FINDING YOUR PLACE

For many of us, even as adults, we struggle to find our place in the world. When your **confidence** has taken a lot of blows, it can make it difficult to carve out your own corner. For most of my life, I kept trying to figure out who I was and how I fit in the world. My career path should have been simple: I got good grades, was a member of the Honors Society in high school, and I should have had the stereotypical path to college and success. But I didn't.

When I was in my junior year of high school, I was promised a financially secure position with a big local company. A man my family knew from church asked me to work for him. I'd be doing some small tasks around the office, he said. He told me not to be concerned with affording, or even attending, college because he would hire me straight out of high school. This seemed like a huge blessing to our family. My parents were retirement age and on a fixed income, so not having to pay for my college education was a massive relief. I believed what he told me, skipped the SATs and the scholarship applications, and went straight to his office after graduating in 1987.

When I got there, I realized he had been lying. He had no say-so in the hiring and, because I had no real experience and no college degree, the company wouldn't even consider me as an employee. This was a devastating blow that completely derailed my self-esteem. Meanwhile, my friends were all leaving for college and I did not have the heart to backtrack and try to go. To admit that I had failed.

I did, however, **resolve** to find my path to success and to not let this setback upset my life for too long. The problem was that I didn't know what I wanted to be. When I was young, I had dreamed of dozens of jobs—designing cards for Hallmark, being a weather girl, a private eye, an artist, a ballerina, or maybe one of the girls in an MTV video. For a while, I even wanted to be a model on *The Price is Right*. But when I went for a modeling audition, I was turned down because of my height. I was told no one would ever want a 5'3" model. Despite all of the naysayers and the closed doors, I was determined to find my path to success.

So I wandered a bit. I tried to find an area that I loved. I spent the first nine years after high school graduation performing a variety of jobs, from cashier to magician's assistant, receptionist to leg model. Finally, in 1996, I got a job at an insurance company and realized this could be a great path for me. A year later, I obtained my Property and Casualty License and finally found a career I could stay in for life. At the time I accepted this position, I really just wanted a daytime job with some stability. The more I learned about the field and how I could really help people, the more **motivated** I became to excel. Ironically, more than one customer referred to me as a "magician" when finding solutions for them. That made me feel good and fed into my desire to help other people.

BE YOUR BEST MERMAID

Being female was often a disadvantage in every industry I pursued, so if I let that stop me, then the bullies would win and I'd be defeated. Both men and women judged me or looked at me as someone incapable of achieving my dreams. Modeling, for example, was an "impossible" goal for me because of my height. Yet I didn't let that stop me from pursuing modeling opportunities long after I was in my early twenties.

Mermaid:

masculine merman, a fabled marine creature with the head and upper body of a human being and the tail of a fish. Similar divine or semidivine beings appear in ancient mythologies. In European folklore, mermaids (sometimes called sirens) and mermen were natural beings who, like fairies, had magical and prophetic powers. They loved music and often sang. Though very long-lived, they were mortal and had no souls.
Source: Encyclopedia Britannica

As women, we bring so much to the world but we often don't see our own value. When we get knocked down, it's our duty to pick ourselves up and proceed with **dignity**. We need to be the shining examples that younger ladies need. I look at the mermaids I started drawing as a young girl, and still draw today, and see in them an example of having strength in their **individuality**. I know they are mythical, legendary creatures, but they are also a symbol of being okay with being different—and it truly *is* okay to be different.

You have to learn to be your own best mermaid. Look at the characteristics that make you different from everyone else and *embrace* the differentiators. Use them to carve out a path and a life that is uniquely yours.

Another tool to use is this: Know in your head what **sincerity** and authenticity look like, then use discernment in all situations and relationships. Anything less than realness from other people does not deserve your attention, and it definitely shouldn't cause heartache. Protect your heart. No one else will. Mermaids do this as a way of life because they only stay in situations that make their hearts happy. They don't get trapped in negative bubbles or dark worlds.

For me, the friends I've had since kindergarten stuck with me, and I with them. We're still friends to this day, and they are the ones who have laughed with me, cried with me, and have given me a hug when I needed it most. They are my examples of true friendship. A real friend is the kind who shares her lunch because you forgot yours or offers to walk your dog because a family member is in the hospital. She is there, no matter what. I try to be that for my friends and am so grateful for all the women who have been true friends to me.

They also supported me when I found out about being adopted and started asking more questions as I got older. When I finally found the answers I had been needing about my adoption, it did help mitigate some of the damage from all those years before. Turned out my answer was practically right next door. When I turned eighteen, my mother finally told me who my birth mother was. I had known my birth mother my whole life as a friend of the family who lived a few hours away.

The first time I remember interacting with her, she was already in her mid-forties. I didn't see the resemblance and later found out that I looked more like my birth father. My birth mother became pregnant when she was forty but she was misdiagnosed with a stomach tumor for the entire first trimester. When she realized she was having a baby, she panicked. It was too late for an abortion and *Roe v. Wade* wasn't decided until about twenty years later. My conception was the result of an affair and she was terrified her husband would find out.

In desperation, she contacted her lifelong friend. My birth mother was suicidal and at the end of her rope because she didn't see a way out of this horrible situation. Her friend begged her not to hurt the baby and promised to raise me as her own. That friend became my mother, who treated me all my life as if I had been hers from the very start. It was gratifying to know that I had been loved by my birth mother all along, and that my life was as a result of two strong women coming together to do the best and right thing for me. They **empowered** each other through support and friendship.

But the biggest lesson I learned in life was to understand who I am through my own eyes. It took years to be able to look at myself without criticism and to see the beauty and value in every part of myself. Too often, we judge ourselves harshly based on the skewed lens through which we view ourselves. It's a lens that is often one that others have conditioned us to use. With perseverance and self-love—things we will talk about in this book—we can overcome the harsh judgments we have learned to impose on ourselves and effectively love others because **we love ourselves**. Be a mermaid and love yourself exactly as you are, even if what you are doesn't fit some predetermined societal norm.

CHAPTER TWO

Swim Like You Can't Drown

When I was in first grade, my mother entered me into a readathon for Multiple Sclerosis because she knew how much time I spent in the library, poring over books. I loved to read, and the contest was a good way to donate to a good cause. Each contestant committed to read a certain number of books in the allotted time. Sponsors pledged a monetary gift per book read.

I wanted to do well and said I would read one hundred books in the six-week span. This was a **challenging** declaration, but I knew how much I loved to read and wanted to try. My mother insisted I approach potential sponsors on my own without her doing it for me so I could learn how to talk to people. But I was five, and the only place I went besides school was church. I was shy and nervous, but I started asking people the following Sunday. I was determined to achieve my reading goal.

Most people I approached were friendly, and they were willing to help. One church member, however, reacted in a way I'll never forget. I worked up my **courage** to talk to him, and as soon as I said I would read a hundred books, he laughed at me and said, "You can't do that!" Just to prove his point, he pledged a ridiculous amount per book because he was counting on the fact that I would fail.

The moment he laughed and doubted me felt just like when those girls who cornered me and made fun of me—that sneer and doubt and the feelings of insecurity it all evoked. The humiliation of his laughter stung, as I was quite the sensitive soul, but his disdain made me more determined than ever. I didn't just read a hundred books—I read a hundred and five. My mother stopped me from reading any more out of respect to the other donors. I must say it felt good to walk up to him and triumphantly collect his pledge. The best part? I raised a nice amount of money for the cause. In fact, I also received the grand prize of a hundred dollars (a fortune to me!) for my endeavor and had the honor of being the youngest student to ever earn that award.

BELIEVE YOU CAN DO IT

The best place to start when you're faced with the thought of failure is with *yourself*. We have to start believing we can do it, even when others undermine us or expect our failure.

In 1979, I started ballet lessons with a very strict director of a ballet company. Even at ten, I was a natural of sorts and I loved it so much. I worked very hard, performed recitals, and within three years, had worked up to pointe shoes. That spring, I auditioned for the big seasonal production and not only landed my first role *en pointe* but also was appointed as an understudy to one of the lead ballerinas. Because my sister attended rehearsals for the whole cast and show, I eagerly tagged along and watched. I quietly memorized all of the choreography. My soul **thrived** in this world, in the excitement and beauty of it.

One day, a lead ballerina—not the one I was the understudy for—ran late and wasn't there in time to rehearse her *pas de deux*. Her male partner needed a counterpart to rehearse the tarantella. I quickly raised my hand to volunteer. The company gave the director skeptical glances, but she said, "Let her do it."

I was passionate and prepared. That makes a difference. The butterflies in my stomach were intense, but I performed the tarantella flawlessly in front of the entire studio, and I even received a standing ovation. I was thrilled; I knew I could do it!

Overcoming Your Fear of Failure

Fear of failure can be extremely paralyzing. Don't let it stop you in your tracks.

- If you fall down, pick yourself up
- Go into an endeavor expecting success
- Remember, the beauty of life is often found in our adventures and those we meet along the way
- Ask yourself what lessons you have learned
- When you feel defeated, consider the success you will miss if you stop trying
- Realize few people get it right the first time
- Take joy in the learning process
- Often, what we perceive as failure leads to something even better

Failures won't define you as a person if you forbid them to!

After class, an older dancer came up to me. "You have guts," she said, "and that's what will get you through." Mustering "the guts" was not always easy because my awkward preteen years were filled with gut-wrenching insecurities.

Many people were surprised I had memorized the choreography without writing it down. What they didn't understand was that I had been using memorization as a coping mechanism for my anxiety for years. I was able to concentrate on the steps I had learned and feel more confident as I performed because I had spent so much time learning the dance.

Outside of ballet class, life was still hard. I was a middle-schooler who was small and looked more like a nine-year-old, so I continued to get picked on at school. Bus rides were excruciating because a couple of really hateful girls from a grade higher sat behind me and taunted me the whole way to school and back. Dealing with this torment was so much more difficult than performing ballet in front of a sold-out coliseum on the University of Kansas campus.

The environment at school was the polar opposite from the ballet world I thrived in and loved so much. At ballet, I was with a group of peers and adults who shared the same **dreams** I did. That helped me realize I had purpose and to see my performance achievements as a way to maintain that belief in myself. Ballet was familiar; this new place was not. I had to work hard to get through each day until I became comfortable and confident again.

No one else can believe in ourselves as much as we can, and we certainly shouldn't try to put that responsibility on anyone. Haters become angry when they see we have the guts to try what they are afraid of, especially when we succeed!

INSECURE PEOPLE LASH OUT AT OTHERS

When I was young, it was hard to see that other people's insecurities were at the root of their cruelty. It's hard not to take being called ugly or stupid personally, especially as women. However, this isn't just an issue among women; men can be just as unkind. Bullying doesn't discriminate. It can come from anyone, anywhere, and at any time.

When I was in my early twenties, I was in a relationship with someone who played in a pool league, so I learned how to shoot pool. It's a primarily male-dominated sport and the local competitions were often held in smoke-filled bars. It was intimidating, but I loved the **challenge** of the game.

When you are shooting pool in a bar, you have to put quarters on the table to "drop the balls" before you begin. If no quarters are sitting on the edge of the table, anyone can walk up and get control of the pool table. If they do, it's an indication of a challenge to the winner of the current game. When we were playing, a man walked over and put his quarters on the table, challenging the winner of our game, thinking he could easily beat us.

I won the game, so I played the over-confident challenger—and beat him. He turned around and called me a slut because I won. I was shocked but sadly, not surprised—it happens far too frequently. As women, we often deal with undeserved hostility from men. His insult spoke volumes about *his* character, not mine. Men like him will sometimes bully women they find attractive because of their own insecurities and fears of rejection. We women should not take any ownership of this hostility towards us, but rather recognize the issue lies within the man who is misbehaving. Remember: *Bullying is never about you. It's about the bully's insecurities.*

Bullies deserve no credibility. Insecurity and fear drive them. Bullies doesn't stop when they graduate from school—they are out in the real world every day. The key is in how you respond.

BE PREPARED TO WORK TWICE AS HARD

I entered the male-dominated field of insurance in 1996. A year after I got my first job, I passed the test to receive my Property & Casualty license for the State of Kansas. When people called the office and I answered the phone, they automatically assumed I had no credibility or knowledge because I was female. I had to work twice as hard as the males in the field to not only prove I was as capable as anyone else, but also just as knowledgeable as any other agent on most insurance matters.

After managing several offices in Kansas and excelling in sales, I decided there was more to life than sitting behind a desk day after day. My husband and I decided to move to Florida, where I had to start over again building my reputation in the insurance world. In this industry, females sometimes tend to be more hands-on, almost controlling and territorial, but a lot of that is because of the uphill battle for equality in this field and in society in general.

Gaining credibility with clients is always initially challenging, especially when working for a male, but I found that setting myself up as **capable** from the start was the best course of action. When a customer tried to insist they wanted to only speak with a male agent, I would say, "You can either wait for a call back from him or resolve your issue now with me." Soon, customers stopped asking for him and wanted to talk to me, which made the boss happy and it allowed me to build my reputation as a problem solver. In my opinion, I think we should all try to be the person others depend on to solve problems. That makes you more valuable.

Since I've lived in Florida, I've started selling artwork, carving out my own little niche while still working in the insurance industry. I have experienced rejection and failures on many levels and in many ways, especially with my artwork, but I keep going because **I believe in myself** and know I can do it.

There will always be those who expect us to fail, but we aren't forced to agree with them. Mermaids know who they are and believe in themselves; they are confident, even though they bridge two radically different worlds.

Just because you aren't living your exact ideal of what you think success is, doesn't mean you aren't successful. Sometimes, it's just the bitter words of the sharks around you that make you doubt yourself. Examine your own moves and motives, especially when you find yourself encountering the same type of shark over and over. As long as you acknowledge there are sharks lurking in the waters around you, you can learn to keep swimming strong and not act like bait.

Meeting and surpassing challenges is the best part of my job despite the obstacles I have faced. I get to be myself and use my skills in studying hard and problem solving to be the best in my arena. Don't change who you are even while swimming amongst the sharks— just find a different way to cross the ocean!

CHAPTER THREE

Hold My Beer

If you put a challenge in front of me, I'm going to take it on. One spring, I was working at State Farm as both a financial products manager and a trainer for customer service and sales reps. Our district manager decided to initiate a sales challenge between the offices to see who could book the most loans.

My manager had been successful at outselling *all* of the other offices he had competed against, beating teams of staff single-handedly by making more sales than the teams in a two-hour period of time. I was determined that my team of three ladies would beat him this time.

At the end of the two hours, I had outsold him based on my sales alone—the additional sales by my teammates were just icing on the cake! Just like the readathon challenge, I didn't want to be told I "couldn't" do something or feel like I was expected to fail. This was different, however, because I knew that I could do it and had no problem saying essentially, "Hold my beer. I've got this." That self-confidence was hard-won over the years, but it has served as fuel when challenges arise.

Hitting the Target

Sometimes we all just need a reminder of the steps we need to take to conquer a challenge. We get nervous or unsure and forget that it's as simple as FISH:

- **F**igure out what you want to accomplish
- **I**nvest in time and discipline
- **S**et up rewards that make you tick
- **H**ave strong boundaries and convictions

THERE IS FREEDOM IN CONFIDENCE

Confidence is built from trying and failing, over and over again. Ballet really taught me those lessons, along with discipline. I also learned early on that **continued**

practice elevates our success, no matter what endeavor we are attempting to accomplish. I spent hours practicing before I could do my first pirouette, and it was years before I could do my first *en pointe*. None of the work I did in ballet came easily or was without sacrifice.

That discipline was a key tool in constructively channeling my energy. None of the roles I accepted were handed to me; I prepared meticulously for every single audition and intentionally tried out for roles that were outside my comfort zone. The competition was tough, but I knew I would never develop the strength and confidence I needed if I stayed within the frame of the things that came easily. Earning a solo meant considerable effort, practice, strength, and confidence—something that I built through every single practice. Through discipline, we can improve ourselves and reach amazing goals.

Performing on stage opened doors I had never imagined would be available to me. My roles as a Spanish dancer, Seraphim, Chinese dancer (and many more) enabled me to step outside myself and become something exotic and fabulous. I learned to explore other cultures, other worlds, and I took great joy in engrossing myself in the parts I danced. In my head, I actually became the sassy yellow doll and the majestic, glittering snowflake; and I performed those parts with all my heart. There was freedom in acting a role and in giving myself that taste of another life. The applause was fantastic validation, and it taught me that **taking chances and exploring the many beauties the world offers liberates us to take risks**.

FOCUS ON THE BIGGER GOALS

When I was a little girl, I would sit down in front of the television as often as I could and watch *The Price is Right*. I watched the models on that show and wanted to be just like them. The first time I auditioned as a model was when I was eighteen—and I was immediately rejected because, at 5' 3", I was too short. I thought my dream was over.

Then, a few years later when I was still living in Kansas, I was approached about doing some leg modeling for a local photographer. I did some print work and appeared in a couple of local commercials, but I thought that was as far as I would go with it and eventually set that dream aside.

This past year, at the age of fifty, modeling opportunities started coming my way! The owners of the shops where my artwork is displayed asked me to model their clothing lines. After that, a number of things fell into place—a modeling group asked me to join them, I was a feature model for an international fashion magazine, and I recently walked the runway for several designers in a show. I also landed several freelance projects, including a national commercial for a leg cream. I am so thankful these opportunities came my way, especially since I've reached an age where I believed any sort of modeling career was impossible.

My friends and family were overwhelmingly supportive, but what disturbed me was the men who construed my photos as an invitation to hook up. Since when did posting a completely appropriate photo on social media turn into a dating site type invite?

It wasn't just the men; some of the feedback from other women was unexpectedly hurtful. To me, posting pictures of my modeling jobs is no different than posting photos of my artwork, yet some women have accused me of posting the images because I want "attention", or I am "shallow", or with everything going on in the world "modeling" is all I "care about". **Ladies, instead of competing, lift each other up**! Support each other, especially when someone is going out of their comfort zone or fulfilling a lifelong dream. It takes no effort to tell another woman that you admire her, or think she's beautiful, or that she's done a great job on a project. Be a force for good in other women's lives, not negativity.

Some of the judgmental comments make no sense to me. Hairdressers post photos showcasing their talent to obtain more jobs, Mary Kay representatives use photos that showcase their products, and there are many more businesses utilizing social media as a marketing tool. Yet a woman celebrating an achievement is seen as self-centered. I'm like any other business—I use those photos as a way to obtain more modeling opportunities, promote the designers, and showcase the talented photographers behind the camera. I think some of it harkens back to some people's bullying tendencies. There is more than enough viciousness in the world and we really need to learn from an early age to celebrate, not denigrate.

I have considered deleting my Facebook page because of the mean people, but I won't. I know exactly who I am, and those who really know me are supportive. I'm proud of what I have accomplished and have no problem celebrating that or celebrating it in other people. My long-range plan is to change minds and support other women. Shutting down my page doesn't accomplish either of those goals. We cannot allow ourselves to be distracted by the haters, instead we must **keep going forward,** pursuing our goals and dreams.

ALWAYS BE CONFIDENT IN WHO YOU ARE

Confidence breeds confidence, so it makes sense to do what makes you feel confident. For instance, wearing dresses and high heels makes me happy and feels normal because I don't feel as short in heels. So many women choose more masculine attire, not necessarily because that's what they prefer but because society has conditioned us against being "girly". Instead, I feel like we should celebrate our womanhood, if that's what makes you happy and feel your best. I refuse to change who I am to fit a society-imposed stereotype. Femininity is not congruent with helplessness or frivolity.

Shiny lip gloss is not an indicator of one's IQ. Just because I wear makeup and glittery nails does not mean I cannot bait a hook, catch a fish, shoot a gun, play poker, or change a tire. I have more than one video of me competing in archery (and beating many of the men) while wearing a cute dress, hoop earrings, and wedge heels!

Be who YOU are, no one else!

I love the movie *Fried Green Tomatoes* for many reasons, but one factor really resonates. The women in the movie each knew who they were, but that knowledge was something that evolved over the years. They were strong in their convictions and found themselves and their place in the world more and more every day.

Some of us are so busy people pleasing and identifying ourselves as a daughter, wife, or mother, that we never really know ourselves as the **individuals** we are. Individual means one, a singular being, and you are more powerful than you know.

Let's not be copycats or conformists. Let's instead embrace the strengths that we have and nurture our inner confidence. That way, the next time someone sets a challenge before you, you'll simply say, "Hold my beer, and watch me succeed."

PART TWO

Patience

CHAPTER FOUR

Make Boundaries a Priority

On land, it seems like most mammals aren't restricted by too many boundaries—they can climb hills or duck into valleys without a lot of trouble. For sea animals, boundaries are just as necessary, even if they don't seem to exist in one giant, connected, water environment. Currents carry food, plants, and larva across the world, and sea life often has to work hard to maintain boundaries that protect their young and their food supply. Boundaries are literally necessary for life in the ocean.

It's the same for us as people. We all need boundaries and personal ethical standards because they allow us to stand up to and deal with the inevitable pressure that comes later in life. Tough choices are a part of being an adult, and we need to know what's comfortable and morally sound to us as we navigate those choices. Practicing such discernment starts with learning to say no.

We also have to understand the **consequences** of the boundaries we set. Sometimes, saying no could mean turning down tempting things like a nicer car, a vacation, or a romantic partner whom we know is not good for us. Even as adults, there can be an element of peer pressure. Saying no can be difficult, especially when you feel rushed, but it's important to know your boundaries and stand firm. Saying no when it's difficult and when people are being pushy means *No* is the correct answer. Take your time, consider all of the important information, listen to your instincts and, above all else, trust yourself. Saying *no* is a matter of self-respect.

Boundaries Evolve Over Time

One important thing I learned when I began establishing boundaries was that they take work and awareness. We can encounter boundary-crossers everywhere we go, so being vigilant and trusting our **discernment** is important.

If you find yourself accommodating others at your own expense, then you have to ask yourself: "Why am

I saying yes to people? Is it out of fear that they will reject/hate/be upset with me or is it some misplaced sense of obligation?" Be honest with yourself—if you aren't, it's very easy to lose yourself in the process. When someone doesn't respect even your smallest "no", that's a good indicator you are encountering a boundary crosser.

When I struggled with setting boundaries, I would find myself at the end of the day wondering, "Why am I always busy but not accomplishing any of my own goals? Why am I so tired all the time?" It took a while to realize I had allowed others to control my emotions and actions instead of saying no. Essentially, I let people walk all over me.

As women, we often don't want to rock the boat or upset anyone. That people-pleasing tendency can easily derail into codependency where all we do is try to please the other person, even at the expense of our own needs. We end up losing ourselves in another person and develop an unhealthy need for that relationship, and for pleasing that person. That kind of attachment opens the door to abuse and victimization. There are people who will quickly take advantage when you are vulnerable.

No matter what happens, remember YOU control how you respond, how you feel, and how you act. Once you let someone cross your boundaries, it's more uncomfortable and more difficult to enforce them after the fact, because women often avoid confrontation. Don't be afraid to stand up for yourself and what's important to you. **It's never too late** to change an unhealthy situation. You have the power to make changes. You hold the keys. Use them.

One way to establish boundaries is to know your values. What's important to you? Honesty? Commitment? Think about and write down potential scenarios where someone might lie to you or let you down, and then think about how you would respond. It's sort of like a role-playing game, only you are preparing ahead of time for the conversations that are necessary to stand up for yourself and your values. This puts you in the power position instead of the victim role.

Remember, you can't be empowered and be a victim at the same time. **Choose empowerment.**

KEEPING CODEPENDENCY IN CHECK

Codependency can be sneaky, and you might not even realize you are being codependent or in a codependent relationship until it's too late. It can show up in the small things—like not listening to classical music or saying you don't like it (when you do) because your partner dislikes it. You don't have to compromise on pizza or room colors or what kind of car you drive just to keep the peace. If the relationship derails when you don't bend to someone else's will, that's a huge red flag.

Yes, compromise is necessary; but there's a big difference between compromise and completely acquiescing. Don't change your opinion or convince yourself you don't like something just for the sake of getting along. Adopting views contrary to your own just to please someone else is the very definition of codependency. You don't have to say you like sushi when you don't. You should always feel like it's okay to disagree about everything from politics to paint colors.

In romantic partnerships, it can be easy to forget that your mate should treat you with the same respect and loyalty as they would a best friend. The rules of being a good person don't change just because you're physically intimate with a person.

In my own life, I know that I would do anything to keep my best friend safe and I know she would do the same for me. We always know where we stand with each other and we give as much, if not more, than we take from each other. That relationship taught me to expect the same kind of loyalty and devotion from the person I chose as my mate. My best friend would never consider verbally abusing me, so why would I allow a partner to do so?

Empowerment comes from sticking to your principles and saying no without apology. No is a complete sentence—you don't have to apologize for saying it. Compromising by being passive undermines your standards and yourself. Know *why* you are saying yes before you do—because you don't want to agree to things that directly oppose your moral code. Doing that chips away at your self-respect and self-esteem, which can lead you down a dark road if you're not careful.

Take a good look at the decisions you make and the interactions you have with other people. If you find yourself in a codependent situation, the first key to healing is awareness. Then find the help you need to make changes. Believe in yourself. **Know your worth**. When you know your worth, it is easy to say no and know exactly why you are doing it.

Saying No in the Workplace

Saying *no* in the workplace can be a lot more difficult than in friendships and relationships because of the impact on your job. However, standing up for yourself can help you gain others' **respect**.

Stereotypes can be harmful and is one of the areas where we definitely need to set boundaries. As women, we shouldn't be expected to make coffee for our male counterparts in the office, clean the bathroom, tidy the break room or kitchen, or wash dishes. We also shouldn't be expected to perform secretarial duties for our peers. When faced with these stereotypes, respect yourself and say no. Remember: **it's completely okay to say no.**

Women sometimes feel the need to prove themselves by taking on extra work. It's hard for us to say no to this because we sometimes fear we are more expendable than our male coworkers. So we put in the extra hours and take on the extra assignments, which can lead to burnout and resentment. For some women, success comes at the cost of their work/life balance and family. Remember what is most important in your life—and show that by making your loved ones and yourself a **priority**.

You can also show self-respect through your appearance—and most importantly, your confidence in yourself. Your self-esteem should never hinge on how good you look. Your appearance at work should be about looking professional, not about seeking approval from your coworkers.

Conduct yourself with dignity and professionalism. That means never using your appearance to curry favor rather than using your skills, talent, and work ethic. Using your appearance to define your identity only leads to heartache, both on and off the job.

Be the Queen of the No

When you are faced with a choice about boundaries, try these steps to evaluate whether you should say yes or no, and how to answer effectively:

- Before answering, consider what you really want or need in that moment.

- Don't allow yourself to be rushed. That's almost always a warning sign of a boundary-crosser.

- Know your core values.

- Practice reinforcing boundaries by saying no to the small things first (the Tupperware parties and extra carpool trips).

- You should never say yes out of a feeling of guilt.

- Weigh the consequences of your answer, whether it's a yes or no. Can you live with those outcomes and know you did the right thing?

- When you say no, don't feel the need to explain your answer. No is a complete sentence.

- Finally, don't settle or compromise your values out of fear. Be the fearless mermaid you were meant to be!

In my early twenties, I worked at a department store during the Christmas rush. The much older head of store security kept hitting on me. He made many sexual advances and I always politely turned him down. At the time, I didn't know to report him. This was before the #MeToo movement and before women felt comfortable speaking up against sexual harassment. He accused me of stealing and I was fired. There was no proof, only the jilted security guard's word. I did go to the general manager and told him what happened. He erased the theft report but he didn't give me back my job.

It never occurred to me that saying no to the security officer's advances might cost me my job. Unfortunately, this type of thing still happens often to women and it also often goes unreported. Women can feel so pressured to comply that they feel they don't have a choice but to succumb to the pressure and keep their jobs.

We have come a long way in how we handle sexual harassment and sexual assault. While more and more women are finding the courage to speak up, expose, and prosecute their offenders, we still have a long way to go. It's important to set those boundaries at work and to stand strong in your convictions. The women who have done so are the roots of the #MeToo movement, and only by standing **strong together** can we change the world.

LEAVE FEAR BEHIND

A fear of rejection can also sometimes motivate us to say yes when we don't want to. We worry that saying no means people won't like us anymore. Or worse, we expect retaliation for our no in the form of verbal abuse or passive-aggressive behavior. Fear is the top indicator that you're being pushed into an agreement you don't want to make. Listen to that feeling in your gut when someone responds inappropriately to you or demands an explanation that says more about their character than yours. Your no *never* needs justification.

When faced with a tough choice, I often think back to how I used to solve mazes when I was a child. Instead of helping the mouse find the cheese, I brought the cheese to the mouse by starting backwards. I apply this concept by mentally putting myself on the other side of the decision by thinking through what might happen if I said yes, and what might happen if I said no.

The next time you're facing a choice, take a second to think about the consequences of either choice. That pause helps shed light on unforeseen or unrealized consequences. If the best answer is no, then use your resolve and unapologetically stick to it.

No is a complete sentence. Always.

CHAPTER FIVE

Recognizing a Frenemy

We talked earlier about the movie *Mean Girls*. There's a reason it's a classic—it contains a universal truth: There are friends and there are "frenemies"—the people who pretend to be your friend but are really undermining, gossiping about, or purposefully hurting you behind your back.

Frenemies are often insecure people who can only feel better if they put someone else down. They're easy to spot in high school because their tactics are sometimes more blatant, like not allowing you to sit at their lunch table or spreading a rumor about you. Adult frenemies, however, have decades of experience and are much better at creating subterfuge, making them easily overlooked. See if you recognize any of these people:

Which Kind of Mermaid Are You?

There are several kinds of mermaids in folklore and legend, each said to have different powers. Some are there for good, others for bad, just like friends and frenemies:

1. **Sirens**: these are the most mischievous, and have the worst reputation (sirens grounded Odysseus's boats and delayed his return home)

2. **Water Nymphs**: these are the guardians of their domain, whether it be sea or lake

3. **Merrow Mermaids**: these British Isle mermaids are tiny, and also called wee mermaids. They are sweet and slightly mischievous

4. **Ceasg Mermaids**: these Scottish mermaids are rumored to have salmon tails. They can be nice, but if they are angered, they will seek revenge

5. **Selkies**: these British Isle mermaids have the ability to shapeshift and walk on land. No matter where they are, they always long for the ocean

- **The Backhanded-Compliment Frenemy**: These are the people who give you a compliment, then undermine those words at the same time. Like: *That dress looks really great on you and look at how it hides that baby weight you still have.* Or: *I loved that casserole, even though you burned it a little.* For a second, you wonder if the person just complimented you or criticized you (hint: they are doing both). You find yourself rushing to apologize, to smooth the waters, instead of saying, "Hey, that was mean."

- **The Keeping-Up-With-the-Joneses Frenemy**: This kind of friend/enemy has to outdo anything you do. If you get a new Toyota, she's out buying a new Lexus. If you run a mile, she says she ran two. If you have an occasion to celebrate, she's blasting her good news. These people struggle to let other people have the spotlight and they'll do whatever it takes to keep it on themselves, including burying your achievements.

- **The Undermining Frenemy**: These are the people who sound like they're supportive, but they're really undermining you. For instance, you start talking about switching careers and your Undermining Frenemy says, "*Are you really sure you want to do that? Isn't that a struggling industry right now? Are you really ready to do something new? Why not stay with* *what you know?"* The Undermining Frenemy whispers all those doubts that make you second guess yourself.

- **The We-Must-Match Frenemy**: These are the kind of women who exclude you if you don't fit in with their version of what's acceptable. If you don't wear the right brands or you aren't vacationing at the right location, they'll exclude you from future events. They make you feel pressure to wear, say, and do the right things. Nobody needs that kind of pressure. Just walk away. Life is not about things; it's about good people, and frenemies are *not* good people.

- **The Narcissistic Frenemy:** These people only want to talk about themselves. They're very self-centered and think everything should revolve around their wants, needs, and moods. They make you feel like your emotional needs are far less important than theirs and that you are being insensitive to their needs. They always ask for favors and make you feel that you should be grateful you are in their presence by minimizing your accomplishments. Keep yourself in check by assessing your relationships so you don't fall prey to the illusion this frenemy creates. These frenemies rarely change, so the best thing to do is just end the connection.

- **The Social Media Frenemy:** Many of us are initially excited when we see friend requests pop up on our social media pages. Unfortunately, we soon learn that some of the requests are from fake profiles or they are real people who really don't care about us; instead, they're rather nosy and friending us just to get in our business. Even worse are the ones who see us as "marks" to try to sell us something or convince us to join their multi-level marketing scheme. Personally, I have accepted many friend requests because I see we have several mutual friendships only to learn that their interest in me was solely to further their own sales agenda. While I believe in online marketing, I don't subscribe to this type of manipulation—and you shouldn't, either. We need to be clear with our intentions in all walks of life and examine our motives. When someone's goal, deep down, is to really help others, you won't find them being manipulative.

Also, when someone comes on strong and tries to inject themselves into your life rather than the natural happy transition that should occur, take a moment to stop and examine the reasons why. The person could be way too needy, or maybe they see something in you that they want to extract or take advantage of. Neither of these things constitute a healthy friendship. When a crime is committed, people say to follow the money when looking for suspects. By the same token, we must consider the motives of those who blaze into our lives wanting to know everything before they even try to get to know us.

- **The Hook-Up Frenemy:** Frenemies are not limited to women. Guys can hide under the friendship guise or networking for business ruse when their actual agenda is purely carnal. They are nice until you dismiss their advances and then you are suddenly met with hostility. Isn't it amazing how someone can appear to like you so much…until you don't comply with their wishes? A true friend would never guilt you into doing something you don't want to, nor would they turn hostile. One thing my battered women's counselor taught me is that a classic abuser will always rush onto the scene trying to 'fix' me and seem to care so much, when all he or she is really doing is diverting attention away from their own darkness. Besides, who wants a relationship based on one person viewing the other as "broken" anyway? Rescuing or fixing another individual is not only not our job, it sets up a seriously dangerous and unhealthy dynamic from the very beginning. Self-awareness of what we have to offer in a relationship makes a much better foundation for a healthy relationship with friends and lovers, as well as in a professional setting. Self-love is not synonymous with arrogance or having a disdain for others. Someone who has a healthy sense of self does not feel the need to puff themselves up or belittle others.

Don't mistake prideful, aggressive behavior as true confidence. That is merely a mask that a tragically insecure person wears to deal with the world. Your job is to concentrate on you; their job is to fix themselves.

- **The Needy Frenemy**: This is a person who needs you all the time and gets pouty and starts laying on the guilt the second your attention goes elsewhere. They make you feel bad if you aren't available right away. Just as with the other types of frenemies, it's not your job to be this person's sole source of support. They have to learn to stand on their own two feet without you acting as their training wheels.

Jealousy can also be at the root of a lot of frenemy relationships. The other person might not even realize they are jealous of your looks or your way with words, or whatever thing you have that they covet. That jealousy sometimes starts as early as preschool, when one child steals the toy another child has instead of learning to share. The kid who has to take all the other kids' toys instead of asking to use them or share them can turn into a jealous adult. If kids don't learn to play nice, and don't learn empathy for each other, they grow into adults who can be mean and self-centered.

Empathy is that core trait which allows you to see the other person's point of view and have compassion for them, and then you take those insights into consideration. For example, maybe you have a friend who feels unnerved by new social situations. A frenemy would just drag her to a party, ignore her protests and nerves, and leave her to flounder on her own. A true friend would take the time to make sure the other woman felt comfortable and was having a good time at the party. She would be her wingman, not her deserter, because she would understand that her friend needed support. A friend is one who overlooks your broken fence and admires the flowers in your garden.

When I was a child, I made a friend in our church's youth group. We became close really quickly and I confided in her about my family's difficult financial situation. Within a month, she had moved on to another friend and betrayed me by sharing my information with others. After that, I was slower to trust or confide in people. I learned that not everyone who wants to be my friend can be a true friend. As you move forward in life, you may need to change your circle of friends. Not everyone around you is interested in seeing you improve.

It takes time and effort to be able to recognize people who are being fake. Some have it down to an art, and it takes really listening to a person to see the candy coating over the reality. These false friends become so skilled, it's like they received an instruction manual in the art of pretense. They can be great at pumping up our egos, then undermine them just as quickly.

That's why it starts with you. You have to love yourself, know your value and your worth, and be ready to stand up to people who don't have your best interests at heart. If you get caught up in the frenemy cycle, take a step back, reestablish your boundaries, and detach from them. It doesn't matter what this person thinks about you—because they don't have your best interests at heart. Invest your time in people who do.

You also have to *be* a **true friend** to *have* true friends. Invest in your friendships—ask questions, pay attention to the details, and be there when a friend needs you. True friendship is a two-way street, and both of you have to travel and meet in the middle. No relationship is ever completely equal, and you should know that you're sometimes going to give more than you will receive. A true friend, however, will remember when you were there for them and they will value that support. Real friends lift each other up. Be the **genuine** friend; you'll attract other genuine people.

There's a great quote by Henry Ford that says, "My best friend is the one who brings out the best in me." That's so true for all of us. Surround yourself with people who make you want to be a better person.

And remember, it's not about who is REAL to your face. It is about who STAYS real behind your back.

CHAPTER SIX

Embrace Your Imperfections

Scroll through Instagram, Twitter, Facebook, or whatever the social media hotspot of the day might be, and you'll see photo after photo of perfect people, with perfect skin, perfect smiles, and perfect lives. Their posts are about how amazing their days are and what great spouses they have, making everyone around them feel like they aren't living up to some impossible, invisible bar.

The thing about social media, though, is that it's all an illusion. Perfection itself is an illusion, a thing we chase and can never, ever catch—because *it doesn't exist*. No one is perfect. No one's life is perfect. And no matter how good the lighting is, no one's skin, house, or hair is totally perfect.

We feel so much pressure to be something that is completely unattainable. That need to be perfect damages our self-esteem and makes us worry about things that don't really matter and that aren't possible.

The First Mermaid Sightings

When Columbus crossed the ocean to find the West Indies, he saw what he thought were mermaids. The gentle, giant-tailed creatures lingered around the boats in shallow waters and were unlike anything they had seen before. Today, we know these creatures as manatees, an endangered species that populates the warm waters of the world.

PERFECTIONISM AS PROCRASTINATION

Have you ever stalled on a project because you wanted it to be perfect? I think pretty much all of us have. I know I do that when I try to conquer something others will see but that I haven't mastered. I'm so stressed about making it perfect that I end up not doing anything at all. That creates more stress…it's a vicious cycle.

Some people hide behind the illusion of perfectionism as a way to avoid producing (what they fear will be) subpar results. Like the builder who spends years on his own house and never quite finishes it because he knows that everyone who comes to his house will judge the work. Or the artist who is always "polishing" his creation, but never exhibits it. They are terrified of being judged and somehow falling short, so they procrastinate and avoid both.

I've seen other people use the excuse of being perfect as a way to avoid situations where they will be uncomfortable. I know people who have turned down promotions or avoided projects because they worried they wouldn't be good enough at the task. They felt like the others involved were all better at it, or better suited. That kind of negative thinking keeps you from taking risks and venturing into new territory.

It's one thing to worry about getting things right (like the old construction adage: measure twice, cut once), but it's another to keep fiddling with something instead of finishing it and **releasing** it into the world. I'm an artist and I know very well that art is messy and imperfect, and yet still incredibly beautiful because of its flaws. If I worried about getting each piece "perfect", I'd never create anything. I have to embrace the messiness and imperfection, and accept that it's part of the process and part of the greatness.

Mermaids are like snowflakes—each is different from the other. There is no "standard" for a mermaid. They are proud of their uniqueness and embrace the fact that they are unlike any fish or human in the world. Their ability to straddle two worlds—without feeling the need to conform to either—leaves them happier and more content than all the fish and humans who try to be "perfect" in their space.

Perfectionism as Control

Some people use perfectionism as a means of control. We've all met those people who criticize everything we do or rearrange the dishes after we put them away, or worse, refuse to let you do anything because you'll do it "wrong". This is just a way of controlling the environment or other people, and it ultimately always backfires.

The world is not meant to be perfect and people aren't meant to do everything right every single time. Like we talked about in a previous chapter, storms happen and tear up that perfectly planted flowerbed or blow stray seeds into your new garden. The results can be **amazing** if you learn to let go of control. One of my friends planted a garden during the pandemic and used some of her neighbor's compost. She measured her rows, planted her seeds, and staked her tomatoes. A few weeks later, a vine appeared, then another, and another. They wound their way through the garden and sprouted into a half dozen watermelons. If she had cut those vines back or dug them up because they ruined her "perfect" garden, she never would have had that beautiful surprise.

People who use perfection for control often criticize others about everything from the way they use a preposition to the way they dress. This causes grief wherever it happens, whether it's at work or in a relationship. It also leaves other people feeling devalued and hurts their self-esteem. This happened to me when I was younger, and it paralyzed me. I constantly second-guessed myself about my choices and decisions. It was only when I realized what I was doing was already perfectly fine that I stopped listening to my criticizer.

You can't please or change someone like that. You also can't take what they say personally. Recognize who you are dealing with and emotionally detach. The only thing we can control is our own response. By choosing to detach, you regain control and avoid getting sucked into the victim mentality.

PERFECTIONISM AS COMPARISON

Sometimes, the most beautiful things in life are found in the **imperfections**. Snowflakes, roses, seashells… so many things in this world are stunningly beautiful, and yet each one is 100% unique from the other. Being unique is what makes us special and what makes us lovable—because love is found in the things that set us apart, not necessarily the things that make us the same. There is no perfect standard for anything in nature, yet we see beauty in Mother Nature every day. We embrace the cool plants and birds and the sunsets that are different every single night because we see the beauty in the differences.

And yet we compare ourselves to other people all the time. This woman has a perfect nose, or ideal body shape, or is the perfect size. We have this invisible standard in our heads that society has put in place and we judge ourselves by that barometer all the time. We don't see the uniqueness and beauty in ourselves— we only see ourselves as a measuring stick against someone else.

Imagine how different the world—and our level of happiness and self-confidence—would be if we loved the unique parts of ourselves? If we saw them as assets, not differentiators?

Butterflies, for example, come in over seventeen thousand different species, in so many colors, sizes, and distinctive markings. All of them are beautiful, but different ones appeal to different eyes. There are people who love monarch butterflies and others who love swallowtails. Butterflies don't worry about their appearance or how they compare to one another. Why should we?

Stop measuring yourself against others—**sparkle** in your own way. Be proud and completely unapologetic for your qualities. Understand everyone possesses different gifts, so appreciate your diverse talents and your strengths and flaws—those things that make you... you. More importantly, celebrate the same in *others*.

When I started my very first insurance job, I was trained by the girl I was replacing. The three days I spent with her were exhausting because she was obsessed with how the paperclips held the paper together, how the desk was organized...essentially, every little detail. I worried that I wasn't going to be able to live up to my boss's standards if that was the way he liked things to be done. It was ridiculously stressful and distracted me from what I should have been worrying about—the level of service provided to our customers.

The first day on my own, my boss called me in, and before I could say the job wasn't for me (because I really wasn't going to master that paperclip system), he said "I don't care which way the paperclips go!" I let out a huge sigh of relief and we both laughed. That went on to be a fantastic job for me and was a great start to my insurance career. I didn't have to worry about being perfect—I just had to be good at my job. That was something I knew how to do!

Once you accept that no one is perfect (except God, if you are a believer), your life gets easier and you are less bothered by other people's opinions. No human being is perfect, and no light or creation is perfect. In God's love, we find true love and true acceptance. We should strive to feel that way about ourselves and everyone we encounter.

The Disorder Danger

Dozens of studies have found links between perfectionism and disorders like anorexia, bulimia, and OCD. There's a fine line between making sure everything is done right and obsessing over every detail or every calorie. There's so much internal chaos that the person uses perfectionism to try to control what is going on inside them. It creates a vicious cycle that can be tough to escape.

LETTING GO AND LOVING MORE

Getting away from perfectionism means being vulnerable. It means being okay with failure. And it means opening up to the people who love you and telling them when we are struggling. Give more grace and have lower expectations; I promise you, your life will be less stressful and your relationships will be better.

No one wants to live a life where they constantly walk on eggshells or worry about whether or not the towels line up just so. It's stressful and unhealthy—ironically, it's unproductive because you pour so much energy into the tiny details. Take a step back and look at the big picture. Is it more important that the carpets be clean or that you spend time playing a game with your kids? Is it more important that you fit some impossible size or that you have a girls' night out with good friends?

There are memes out there that say things like, "Eat the dessert because life is short." That's so true. Do you really want to get to the end of your life fitting into some ridiculous size without ever enjoying a slice of cheesecake or apple pie? Life is short—enjoy it and enjoy yourself.

You have to let go of other people's standards and **embrace** yourself as you are. I know how hard this can be because modeling is a world filled with flaw-noticing. My smile is not the gleaming white, perfectly straight, movie star look, nor is my nose the epitome of Hollywood standards. To some people, I'm not perfect enough or tall enough to model. I've chosen to embrace those "imperfections" and enjoy my modeling career.

In the end, outward beauty is fleeting and temporal. When we want deep, meaningful relationships, we must be deep and meaningful within ourselves and concentrate on the inner self, not the outer dressing. That's where true happiness and contentment lie, believe me. Don't play in the shallows and expect to find what only dwells in the deep!

PART THREE

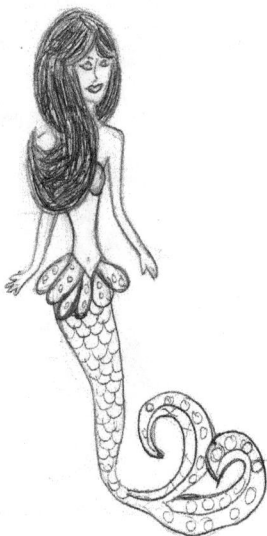

Kindness

Chapter Seven

Make Your Own Sunshine

My mother used to tell me that there would be days when you have to make your own sunshine. When I was younger, I thought that was a silly saying. Growing up in Kansas where winter lasts six months, it was easy to get depressed when the cold, gray days seemed to never end and making my own sunshine definitely didn't seem possible. I would try to look for some ray of happiness, even if I was sure spring and summer were never going to arrive. Yet my mother persevered in her optimism, and I couldn't help but go along with that attitude. My mother was strong, and her model of strength and **resilience** greatly influenced who I am today.

So, take a page from my mother and do the same thing she told me to do. You have to make your own **sunshine**, not just for yourself but for everyone around you, too. If you can learn to make the best out of the worst situations, you end up not depending on anything or anyone other than yourself to make things better. You don't get as irritated or depressed over small things because you see the sun peeking out from behind the clouds. Even with simple things—if someone cuts you off in traffic and you end up late for an appointment, which sends the whole day into chaos—learning to look for the bright side will ease that stress.

Be the Ray of Sunshine Others Need

Sometimes, the easiest way to find sunshine is to *be* the sunshine yourself. When you reach out to other people who are having a bad day, or struggling in some way, that generosity and joy rubs off on you, too.

Think of your friends and family—is there someone you can reach out to today to give them a hug or just a shoulder to lean on?

LEARN FROM THOSE AROUND YOU

My adoptive mother grew up in the middle of Kansas, the youngest of four girls during the Great Depression. Food was rationed. Kansas was always being hit by some kind of natural disaster including floods, blizzards, dust storms, and tornadoes. It wasn't the happiest childhood a kid could have. She went to a one-room schoolhouse that burned down, a moment that was devastating to her because she loved that school. It seemed like everything was against her from the start.

Then, in 1950, she nearly died giving birth to her first-born daughter. When the doctors told her that she might not live to see the birth of her child, she told them to save the baby, not her. When she was recovering in the hospital, her small-town community rallied around her to help because she was still so weak. Strangers lined up to donate blood and others stood outside her hospital room, praying for her. My birth mother actually did code during labor, but they were able to resuscitate my her and she went on to raise my older sister.

Her marriage was rocky, and although she and her husband had three children, she wasn't happy. She ended up having an affair, which is how she got pregnant with me, and she gave me up when I was eleven days old. My adoptive mother already had children, but she wanted to help her friend and said she would raise me as her own.

My adoptive mother, Millie, was one of the sweetest people I've ever known; yet she was, without a doubt, a fighter. She was kind and fun, and many were surprised to discover there was a very strong person who could weather anything that life threw at her under that seemingly soft exterior. She never gave up. If she had, I wouldn't be here. She taught me that being **kind** and **fierce** can coexist.

The adversity my adoptive mother experienced and the way she maintained a positive attitude taught me the importance of being a ray of sunshine to others, even when there are clouds in your own life. She was a woman of action who did this in her everyday life. She lived a life of example for me and my siblings. She would bring us kids along with her to visit people in nursing homes. If my mother found out someone she knew was in the hospital, then we took meals to their families. I remember sitting down with a widow and comforting her in her loneliness. I also have fond memories of the strangers we invited to join our family's Thanksgiving dinner. That was my mother—giving and kind, no matter what was going on in her own life.

If my mother found people who could benefit from good works, we did what we could for them. Sometimes it was as simple as picking up their trash or helping them with yardwork. My mom led the charge for all my siblings and I to see the importance of this **"charity of spirit"**. This influenced how I wanted to pay it forward for others as I got older. She taught me about paying it forward, and about being honest and supportive to those around me.

That's not to say that we never struggled. To stick tightly to her budget, my mother almost always paid cash for whatever we needed, and even though we had all the necessities, there were many times when I envied what my peers had. But she gave what she could and took care of us all to the best of her ability. In some ways, I was richer than anyone else for being so loved by my mother.

BRING YOUR OWN WEATHER

There are people I know who surrendered and became a product of the "weather", meaning their circumstances. Not everyone had a role model like I did in my mother. I learned early on not to be influenced by the shadows in life, but rather to always look for the sun beyond the storms. Some of us, however, get caught up in the doom and gloom and can't see past the bad day, bad week, or bad month. You don't have to become the clouds. You don't have to become your economic situation. You don't have to become your job or the negative people around you.

Even if it's a cloudy day, you can be a ray of sunshine. Yes, people go through hard times. Poverty, loss of a loved one, health issues—but no matter how bad things get, there is always one thing to celebrate and see joy in, even if it's just the breath in your lungs. Gratitude is the key to finding happiness, no matter what happens.

Stop for a second and list ten things you are grateful for. It can be something simple like the shade of a tree on a hot summer day or the cake your neighbor baked for your birthday. Gratitude isn't about the size of the blessing; it's about being thankful for everything you have in your life. Today, list ten; tomorrow, list another ten. If you make gratitude part of your daily life, you will notice that your attitude changes and becomes sunnier.

Learn to make the best of everything you have in your life. Don't depend on others to make you happy, depend on yourself to cheer up a bad day instead. Even better, help cheer up someone else. If there's one thing I learned in my childhood, it was that helping others made me feel ten times better about myself.

When I was in middle school, my mother and I baked nine hundred cookies to mail to the Great Lakes Naval Base. Originally, we wanted to send cookies to my brother who was in Navy boot camp. When we reached out to find out how to get cookies to him, we were told we could not send cookies just for him, we had to send them to all his fellow recruits. Making and sending this huge batch of cookies was an experience I will never forget, and one I'm proud of because I know how much it meant to the sailors far from home. I also learned that

persevering, no matter the amount of time, effort, or money it took to get a task done, was worth it.

Superpowered Mermaids

Mermaids are rumored to have four different superpowers:

- **Immortality**
- **Seeing the Future**
- **Telepathy**
- **Hypnosis**

How they use them depends on what kind of mermaid each is—the more malicious mermaids use these powers to control and manipulate, while others use them to help and support. Sort of like people!

At the time I'm writing this book, we are several months into the 2020 COVID-19 quarantine. During this time, more than ever, "sunshine" is required. For some people, this time could be likened to what my mother went through during the Great Depression because of job losses, food shortages, and the inability to see loved ones. Sunshine was needed then and is needed now to combat the news we hear every day.

To beat the negativity all around us, I try to give my own sunshine out in creative ways, like paying for peoples' Starbucks, picking up groceries for those who can't get out, and taking medicine to a sick friend. I once saw a woman feeding a stray cat at the coffee shop I went to every morning. One day, I handed her a bag of cat food, just because. She was surprised and stunned at that simple act of **generosity**.

I didn't expect anything, not even a thank-you in return, because that's not the way we should spread light among other people. True kindness is not concerned with the outcome and shouldn't be about what we get in return. This is the same thing as pretending to take a genuine interest in someone when you are actually just trying to sell something or get something from them. Be real, be yourself, and most of all, do as Gandhi once advised (I'm paraphrasing) and be the example you want to see in the world because that's how the world changes.

Our hearts are not measured in dollars and cents, nor does kindness have a price tag. Sometimes what we consider a very small act of kindness creates a magnificent impact on the other person and the ripple effect passes that grace on to many others. It can be one moment that turns everything around for them, even if it's just a hug during a really trying time in their lives.

Now that my mom has passed away, I've made it my mission to carry on as she would have. I look for sunshine in the clouds and am kind to as many people as I can. An act of kindness can come from anyone, at any time, and in any form. True **sunshine** costs nothing!

CHAPTER EIGHT

Stay a Fish Among the Sharks

Some breeds of fish, like tuna and herring, spend their entire lives in a school and get agitated if they lose track of the group. Schooling is used as a defense mechanism against predators, as well as a way to hunt and travel faster. Fish don't break out of the school because they know danger awaits any fish who goes it alone.

Humans often do the same thing. We go along with everyone else instead of taking risks and being **unique**. It's far easier to be the same as everyone else and not draw attention to ourselves than risk ridicule or criticism.

We all know there are sharks out there, circling and waiting to point out our mistakes. They're the people with the cutting remarks in the office or the ones shooting others judgmental looks in the store. They're the people who tell you that you can't, or shouldn't, or won't be able to achieve your dreams.

You Can See "Real" Mermaids

At Weeki Wachee Springs in Florida, mermaids are rumored to live in the enchanted waters. A "real" mermaid show has been performed in a giant water tank in front of hundreds of people since 1947. These talented women can hold their breath for an insanely long time!

DON'T BECOME THE SCHOOL

It's easy to fall into the predictable patterns around you. How many people end up repeating the lives their parents and grandparents had? It takes conscious effort to step outside predictable patterns. Although I was exposed to people who abused drugs and were drug addicts, I never turned into one because I was determined not to live that sort of life. It was a conscious effort, every single day, to be different and not end up part of that particular school of fish.

Pay attention to the people who actively try to change you, whether that's in subtle or obvious ways. They're trying to mold you into a person other than the one you were meant to be, maybe because it's more comfortable for them to be surrounded by people just like them (like the tuna and herring). You have to dig in and protect who you are because that person is precious and unique. That kind of manipulation by others can be tough to see, so trust those who love you when they speak up. I've seen people who have been through this and they didn't listen to advice. I wish they had opened their eyes so they would not have been victimized.

The other kind of manipulation is sneakier and more prevalent—advertising and social media put tremendous pressure on women to conform to what society decides is beautiful and perfect. It's hard not to believe that wearing the right brands or driving the right car can make our lives better, or that the people who have all those things are somehow happier. Advertising people are masters at convincing us that the label on our backs is part of the elusive key to joy.

That "grass is greener elsewhere" message seems to be the main image you find in every social media post. All we hear and see is that we must change ourselves to be one of the cool kids. It's perpetuated by reality television and brand marketing. Don't be swayed by all that. Realize that a lot—if not all—of that is part of a carefully curated image. To me, it's exhausting to be that perfect all the time and worrying so much about appearances and other people's impressions.

That kind of image manipulation even happens in the workplace. Sometimes, when new management comes in, there are always a few people who contort themselves to become what they think will help them fit into the new environment. The ones who are **confident** in themselves and their abilities don't worry about that. They just keep working hard and doing their jobs because they know their true strengths.

The key to avoid getting sucked into this craziness is to focus on your strengths in the workplace and shine extra bright with those. Of course, everyone has areas that need improvement, whether it's punctuality or organization. Know where you can be better and try a little harder in that area every day; and be confident in what you do well, whether that's networking or leadership or details. Simply be the best version of who you are, whether you are at work, at home, in relationships, or in the far reaches of the sea.

Combine Independence with Kindness

One of my earliest memories from childhood is insisting to my mother that I could put my Cap'n

Crunch shirt on all by myself. I was three years old and determined to be **independent**. My mother even noted that in my baby book, adding that I "had a very soft heart" even though I was sure I could handle things on my own.

You can be independent and take your own path, and not be mean or arrogant about it. Flying solo doesn't mean you have to be callous or cold. Leaders can take the reins, but they can still be kind and gracious to those around them. Independence can be a part of being a good person to others. Some of the greatest leaders in the world have had that soft side to them, whether it's reading to children or building wells in Africa. Many of them are quiet about their charitable acts because they don't derive satisfaction from public kudos.

Some of us struggle to find our path. Try to think about the things that make you happy, that fill your soul and make you want to charge forward as a leader.

By knowing yourself, you prevent being shepherded into a category, career, or relationship by other people. I've always bristled when people have tried to control me or tell me what to do. Because I'm petite, I think people mistake my size for weakness, but they find I'm quite the opposite when they try to boss me around. I'm strong in my convictions but try to be giving and compassionate at the same time.

I knew a woman at work who, for whatever reason, really didn't like me. Every time I went to the local coffee shop, I asked her if she wanted a coffee—not to try to butter her up, but simply because that's what I do when I get something for myself; I ask if the other people want something, too. A dozen times, she refused me, and then one day she asked me to bring her back a caramel latte. She thanked me and we chatted a bit. We never became great friends, but it thawed whatever wall was between us. I didn't want there to be tension in the office, so I kept throwing out that olive branch until she took it.

In the movie *Legend,* there's a woman who loves to dance, and when the devil wants to capture her for his own, he plays a song that makes her dance so much she begins to forget the world around her. The faster she dances, the more she transforms and gives into the dark forces, eventually becoming something entirely different from who she was. I think of this analogy whenever I feel the pressure to change who I am, even if it's only in a small way.

I learned this lesson with my art as well. For a long time, I tried to create pieces that I thought others would like; yet my art wasn't selling the way I thought it should. I visited the Dali Museum one day and had an inspirational and **pivotal** epiphany: Dali painted from his true self, his own imagination and dreams, and he was never concerned with who would like his creations.

Dolphins might swim in pods, but they are also fiercely independent. They're not scared of sharks, because they defend themselves by hitting the shark on the chest with their tails. This hard strike can literally catapult the sharks far away.

I wanted to be like Dali and could feel the energy and excitement to create building inside me as I left the museum. The next pieces I created shone with personality! Sales picked up and a new journey began. I learned how to lead in the area that I loved and to make it a reflection of my true self.

BEWARE OF THE PREDATORS

There are always going to be sharks in the water, both literally and figuratively, who are looking to take you down a notch or two. The key is figuring out which people are the sharks who wish to do you harm. Take a step back and evaluate a few things:

1. Is this person a negative influence on me?

2. Do I change my behavior in negative ways when I'm around this person?

3. What intentions does this person have for
    their actions?

4. Am I being true to my own nature when I am
    with this person?

The answers to those questions can help you pinpoint a shark. Not everyone is going to like us as we are and not everyone will benefit our lives. Sharks will be sharks, but we don't have to participate in their predatory behavior. Even more importantly, we don't have to lose ourselves in the process. Once you truly know yourself, you can more clearly see the path ahead and which people fit that journey...and which don't.

If you see a woman who is struggling to find her way, consider being a mentor. You're not trying to re-shape her, but rather **elevate** her by helping her maximize who she already is. The best mentors use encouragement and support to help their mentees realize their full potential. Be that for someone else, today!

Chapter Nine

Embrace the Rainbow

Did you know that rainbows are actually optical illusions? They may seem like something you can reach out and touch if only you journeyed far enough (and a pot of gold at the end would be a bonus). In reality, they are a miraculous image created by light refraction and raindrops—almost like a mirage in a desert. Yet, they are something that brings us joy and hope, and they give us a reason to believe things can be amazing again once storms pass.

I've always loved rainbows and see them as a symbol that everything will get better, even after the darkest of days. To me, they represent hope and a reminder of the beauty that can be found after an upheaval. Part of what I love about being an artist is seeing all the amazing colors in this world and finding unique ways to bring them together. I can never duplicate the striking simplicity of a rainbow, but I can try to bring some brightness to the world in my own way.

NOTHING IS BY ACCIDENT

Even though they are considered illusions, I believe rainbows are deliberate; therefore, they too have a purpose, even if it's simply to brighten a stormy day. So many of us struggle and wonder about our purpose for being on this earth. I know that I did, especially given my birth story. I wondered about being unwanted by my birth mother and struggled to fit in with my peers. As I grew up, though, I began to see that everyone has a purpose and every single one of us matters to another person. I mattered to my family, and I mattered to my birth mother. They did everything they could to ensure I had a good, rich life.

So often, we go through our lives barely aware that the small moments and most innocuous-seeming interactions with others can have huge impacts. Give a woman in the grocery store a compliment or let someone go ahead of you in line, and those small kindnesses can make a big difference for the other person. You don't know if that woman was having a really bad day, or if she was late to pick up her kids, or if she was just overwhelmed by work—and that tiny favor may remind her there is good in the world and in the people around her.

Stones from Mermaid Tears

The gemstone aquamarine, a swirling beautiful stone of blues and greens, is said to be made from the tears of mermaids. Part of the mineral species beryl, aquamarine is often found embedded in granite rocks.

There could be a reason you felt inclined to help her in that moment, something you don't even know or realize. So much that happens in our world is not solely about us—but rather about the other lives that are touched in those moments. I remember a woman I met in a store who was strikingly beautiful. I can be shy, especially with strangers, but I felt compelled to tell her how beautiful she was and how gorgeous her outfit was. She started to cry, saying she'd had a really terrible day and that my compliment turned that bad day around. It was a small moment for me, but a huge moment for her.

Go ahead and tell the stranger you like her necklace or that her kids are adorable, or whatever you feel nudged to say. We might not even be aware of our purpose or our impact on the other person. Just have faith that you belong here and matter to others, and that what you say and do matters—a lot.

As women, we are tasked with supporting each other. It's only through the strength of numbers that women have created change, like having the right to vote and the inception of the #MeToo movement. We shouldn't bring each other down—we should try to be a rainbow in others' lives, as trite as that might sound.

Whenever I speak to a group of women, I try to be positive and inspiring. I have no idea if my words make a difference, but I hope that each of them leaves and does something fantastic or pays it forward to the next person. Your impact does not have to be large to be important or to have a fabulous ripple effect that spreads that grace farther than you could ever imagine.

LOVE THE DIFFERENCES

I have a really good friend who is creative, like me, but works in engineering. We differ politically and have very diverse opinions, but we are able to put those disagreements aside and concentrate on our friendship. Our creativity brought us together and that's what is at the base of our friendship. We have an unspoken agreement to avoid discussing politics and enjoy each other's company without judgment. We all need to learn to do that more often.

Just because you don't think exactly the same as another person doesn't mean you can't be friends. It's the differences that make us interesting, just as the variety of colors in a rainbow make it unique and awe-inspiring. Can you imagine what our world would look like if there were only one color? How would a rainbow would appear if it was only red or yellow? Differences create beauty.

If you think about it, it takes millions of water droplets to come together and create one beautiful arc. It takes all of us to come together and make a beautiful world— so be a part of the beauty, not the storm clouds. Be the person who sees the bright colors in the world and teaches the color-blind how to embrace everyone.

The big picture has gotten lost and forgotten in the middle of people feeling the need to be right or to fit in with others. So many events in my life have reminded me what's most important—and I can tell you, with certainty, that it's not the politician anyone votes for or the zip code they live in. I am a domestic and sexual abuse survivor and have suffered PTSD from a house fire and a car accident. I lost my dad to cancer and then lost my mother to flagrant negligence at her assisted living facility. Although it was two years ago, a piece of me is still sitting at her graveside, unable to leave and wondering how I could go on without her.

Those difficult times taught me that the meltdowns over an incorrect Starbucks order or a long wait in traffic are pointless. Not everyone feels that way, something you can see everywhere you go. It's as if people are looking around, trying to find fault for every single thing that doesn't go as expected. The best moments get overshadowed by all that anger and frustration. How fun is that? It's not—at all—and it's definitely not the kind of spirit that fills a rainbow.

It takes a concerted effort to not only survive but to forge ahead and spread light across the world, and to see how truly amazing we all are. As long as we are breathing, we have the opportunity to do that.

Blur the Divisions

A rainbow's colors have no separation between them. It's difficult, if not impossible, to see where one color starts and the other ends. People, like rainbows, should have no divide; we should accept our differences and similarities and blend them between us.

Reproducing a rainbow on canvas can be difficult (I know that firsthand because I've tried many times) because those seamless, blurred lines never look quite as perfect as they do in real life. It's almost poetic, the way the colors blend together yet each color is distinct and beautiful.

As women, we need to remember that whatever color we are is distinct and beautiful. There should be no divisions based on the color of our skin or height or eye color. We are all women—and we should embrace each other and lift each other up, especially when one of us is struggling. When you're in the midst of a difficult time, it can be tough to see the light at the end of the tunnel. That's where you can come in and help a friend (or stranger) look up and see the rainbow that's just waiting above them. You've got that outside perspective that can shine some positivity when it's needed most.

So many voices are speaking up now about the importance of embracing diversity. I think that's fantastic and long overdue. The world is so incredibly unique, which is part of what makes it amazing. How boring would the ocean be if every fish was the same? It would cripple the ecosystem and upset the way Mother Nature works. The universe works *because of diversity*, because of the uniqueness of plants, animals, and people.

The Perfect Arrangement

In my artwork, a rainbow has always difficult for me to reproduce, as I said. The seamless lines between each color make it difficult to blur just the right amount to keep it looking natural. God's rainbow, however, is clearly masterful. The seamless colors blend together in poetic arrangement. Part of that rainbow is all of the people who live in this world He created.

It's the same with our inner selves. We all have so many different qualities—whether it's friendliness or empathy or a sense of humor—which are all part of a bigger master plan, blending us into the people we are today. We are here to complement each other, to bring out the best in this person and that one and then supplement it with our best features. Maybe I'm the violet and you're the green, and that woman over there is the yellow in the world. When we all come together, we create something pretty incredible.

I've always liked Shakespeare's play, *A Midsummer Night's Dream*, which is all about not judging people on their looks. Shakespeare talks about how people tend to fall in love with what they see on the outside, instead of with the amazing person inside, and he used comedy as a way to show us the fallacy of doing so. Shakespeare wrote, "Love looks not with the eyes, but with the mind."

When we have true love for others, we see their *inner* beauty. Too often, we don't have that same true love for ourselves and we criticize everything on the outside. *My hips are too wide, my nose is crooked, my hair is too dry*. How many of us do that to ourselves every single time we look in the mirror?

You're looking in the wrong place.

Don't look in the mirror for validation and support. Look *inside* yourself, right now, and see all the beauty that makes up who you are. Your love for others, your compassion, your sensitivity…all of those qualities are part of the rainbow that makes you who you are.

Are you having trouble doing that? Don't feel bad. Lots of people do. Take a moment to list five good qualities you have. We all have qualities that make us beautiful to others. Knowing and being confident in what you have will transform your life, I promise.

Acceptance is about embracing others. We should embrace the people around us and see the good person beneath the exterior, then turn right around and do the same with ourselves. Stop judging what you see in your reflection because that's not the true you. Set aside your issues and judgments about others, about yourself, and simply see the rainbow that is already in front of you!

You're beautiful and unique. Know that and believe it!

CHAPTER TEN

Write Your Own Fairy Tale

Sometimes all you need to change your life and find yourself living in the fairy tale you've always dreamed of, is a few simple words. Write them down on sticky notes and put them on your bathroom mirror or in your car, and then use them to inspire you to become the person you were meant to be. Here are some of my favorites:

1. **People with passion will rule the world.** Passion is that compelling emotion that is the foundation of everything. Possessing such fervor is a key motivator for succeeding in this world because it makes you excited to face each new day. Don't sit back and wait for

opportunities to fall into your lap because, before you know it, those opportunities will have passed you by. Live life with gusto and take risks to experience as much as you can. The Scorpions have a song called "Make it Real". The lyrics are inspiring. "If you take life as a crazy gamble/Throw the dice take your chance/You will see things from a different angle..." Passion gives you the courage to throw those dice and see where you end up!

2. **No one else's opinion of me determines my self-worth.** Does it really matter what other people think? It shouldn't. There are studies that say people only think about another person for nine seconds before their thoughts go back to themselves. Nine seconds is a blip of time. Are you really going to let that color your view of yourself? Don't listen to their negativity or their criticism. Know that you are valuable; you were made for a purpose and everything about you is amazing.

3. **We are not defined by what someone says about us or our dreams.** Some people try to discourage us from pursuing our dreams because they are either satisfied with being complacent in their own lives or scared to fail, so they're envious of us taking a chance. Had I listened to my naysayers and given up on modeling, art, and radio, I wouldn't be writing

this book now, nor would I have experienced many incredible adventures. Fear keeps you inside your comfort zone instead of bravely stepping outside it to make things happen. Don't let anyone talk you out of your dreams. Just charge forward and take those risks!

4. **Be prepared to handle the next opportunity.** Nobody gets to their destination by sitting in the driveway and waiting for the road to come to them. If you want to take that next step, you have to develop a vision, lay the groundwork, and start moving toward it. Research, work on yourself, and make your wants and needs known so you are ready when that opportunity knocks.

5. **Everyone makes mistakes—forgive yourself and don't look back.** Remorse is a necessary emotion but continuing to shame yourself for a mistake is unhealthy and unproductive. No one is perfect. *No one.* We forgive the people we love far easier than we forgive ourselves. Treat yourself like your best friend—with a loving, kind, and gracious heart.

6. **Work on your relationship with God (or whatever your higher power may be) and keep yourself full.** It's very easy to let insecurity and doubt carve a hole in your chest, a hole many people fill with drugs, alcohol, shopping,

relationships, etc. If you are already fulfilled, you won't be susceptible to feeling a need to fill that void with other people. Addictions to sex, work, alcohol, pornography, drugs, or gambling, can get out of control because the temporary satisfaction gained proves to never be enough. Be honest with yourself. Know your own truth and your value. Live your life from truth and you will survive everything.

7. **Don't worry about the finish line; run the best race you can.** Don't focus so much on coming in first or last in a race. It's the journey that's the best part, not the finish line. Work hard and know that everyone reaches their goal at different points in time. Just because you achieve your goals at twenty or thirty or seventy doesn't make it any less of an achievement. Listen to God, and your subconscious, to keep you moving forward at the pace you were meant to move at.

8. **Believe in your dream for yourself with all your heart.** When we grow up, sometimes we stop daydreaming. We stop believing in the impossible. Take a moment today to just daydream about your future. Whether you see yourself touring Italy or running your own company, I want you to see it, feel it, taste it, and know that it can and will happen. When you believe, you can achieve.

9. **Find and know your purpose.** Every single one of us has a purpose, a reason for being in this world. It doesn't have to be fame or fortune, it can sometimes be as simple as being there for someone else who needs a friend. You have purpose, and you touch lives every time you come into contact with someone else. Believe in that and strive to be kinder, more giving, and more grateful. It's in those quiet moments of strength and charity that we find ourselves and our purpose.

10. **Come from a place that is centered on God and His word.** Agape love is a pure love, without malice or jealousy. 1 Corinthians 13 tells us, "*⁴ Love is patient, love is kind. It does not envy, it does not boast, it is not proud. ⁵ It does not dishonor others, it is not self-seeking, it is not easily angered, it keeps no record of wrongs. ⁶ Love does not delight in evil but rejoices with the truth. ⁷ It always protects, always trusts, always hopes, always perseveres. ⁸ Love never fails.*" (NIV) And that kind of love is how we should treat others and how we should love ourselves.

11. **Take a breath; it's all going to be okay.** I know how hard it can be to pause and breathe when you're feeling panicked; your stomach is in knots and you don't know what to do. Stop whatever you are doing and just take a few really deep, really slow breaths. Close your

eyes and concentrate on nothing other than breathing. Whatever hardship or storm you are enduring today, you have endured before and you can and will triumph. Never give up. Only you have the power of responsibility to move your life forward. So, take a deep breath and know it will all eventually work out.

12. **Never stop trying.** There's a saying about falling seven times and getting up eight, because that's where success is found. Toddlers do this when they're learning to walk—they fall down over and over again but they still keep getting up and trying to take that next step. Success is a process. It's one step at a time, sometimes taking detours and sometimes heading in the wrong direction, but always—always—take that next step. Have the energy of intention to fuel you when you fall down.

13. **You are what you believe about yourself.** If you ever wonder why the same types of people keep crossing your path, it's time to take a step back and look at yourself. Maybe what you are projecting into the world isn't aligned with your heart. Maybe you're stuck in a cycle of shame or feeling like a victim. You can decide to stop sabotaging yourself and make every day going forward different than the days before. With confidence and faith, you will get there. Believe in yourself and in your amazingness!

14. **Live in the NOW, instead of in the rearview mirror.** It's impossible to drive a car down the road if you're constantly staring into the rearview mirror. You wouldn't do that to get from home to the grocery store, so why are you doing that with your own life? Your life's rearview mirror does have some glory days, but it also has regrets and guilt. Don't look at that—you aren't going that way. You are going forward.

15. **Have fun.** Remember to play! Just as mermaids frolic in the bubbly surf, find your way to play and enjoy life. We need more laughter in our lives, so hang out with positive people, watch funny movies, or play happy music in your house. Some of us forget how to relax and enjoy life's pleasures, but unwinding is necessary to refill your well. You can return to whatever challenge you are facing refreshed and ready to conquer!

16. **Cure that "disease to please".** You can't please everyone, no matter how much you want to. That's great news because the only one you really need to please is yourself. So say no to the birthday parties and Tupperware sales, say no to that uncomfortable friend who puts you on the spot, and say yes to what makes your heart happy. Your house doesn't need to be perfect, your hair can be a mess, and you can wear yoga pants every day if you want to.

You can make messy art or paint your roof purple—it doesn't matter. You only need to do what makes you happy and fulfilled.

17. **Turn your wounds into wisdom.** I think that failure is God saying, "Excuse me, you're moving in the wrong direction. Let me correct your course." Sometimes things don't work out and doors become closed to you. You might not understand why that job didn't happen or that relationship ended, but if you look back, you'll see there were lessons and benefits in that redirection. Sometimes hardships happen in order to equip us with the skills we need for the future. Maybe you endured something awful to be the voice of wisdom for another person who is struggling. Don't look at course corrections as anything other than learning experiences and new paths that lead to even better destinations.

18. **Don't force your goals.** When you are pursuing your true passion, it should be like breathing because it comes so naturally. Don't try to force yourself to fit in or accomplish goals that don't match who you are at your core. You can tell if you are working your passion because you would do that job for free. That's where you will find happiness and satisfaction. You don't have to live up to anyone else's standards. Just your own.

19. **Expect to be respected.** You can't demand respect or tell people they have to respect you, but you can conduct yourself in a way that shows you expect to be respected. You don't have to tolerate behavior from others that is belittling, uncomfortable, or mean. You can simply walk away and put up your boundaries.

20. **Your legacy is found in every life you touch.** Find a way to serve, whether it's as simple as paying for someone else's lunch or working at a food bank. Service helps you take the focus off yourself and put it on giving back to others, which in turn enriches your own life. Even one tiny extension of love could be just what someone needed that day to restore their faith and keep them from giving up. Choose to become a messenger of light, not darkness. Be kind whenever possible. Solve problems, don't create them. And be grateful for every part of your life.

21. **Stop comparing yourself to others.** You are as unique as each snowflake is different from the other. I think that's really cool! No one person on this earth is exactly like another, not even twins. We each have our own strengths, weaknesses, and gifts that make us wholly original. So, stop trying to imitate others. Sparkle in your own way.

22. **Surround yourself with great people**. If you want to be a great person, keep a group of great people around you. The kind of people who will fill your cup until it runs over. The kind of people who want you to succeed, who see your amazingness, and who love you as you are. Then turn right around and do the same for them!

If there's one overall message I want you to take from this book it's this: **Love yourself as you are.** You are uniquely and brilliantly made, and you are here for a reason. Love your inner mermaid and let her sparkle in the sunshine!

Feb 12 – 1934   5 yrs 10 mo. 11 d.

Doris Mildred Warren

THE NUTCRACKER
December 17 & 18, 1982

My first Nutcracker as a Mechanical Doll

Glamour with photographer Todd Pillars

Hitting the runway for Whiz Fashion magazine 2020

Love bass fishing!

Always hoping to fly

Show stopper in KC

Mermaids in pink

For more of Paulee's wisdom and story, listen to her show, "Eat, Shop, and Play" on WTAN Talk Radio 1340 AM and 106.1 FM.

Her beautiful illustrations and whimsical seashell art are available in local stores, and also at: http://pauleemermaid.com

Find her on LinkedIn, Instagram, Twitter, and Facebook @Paulee Brandt Bowin

Do You Want to Make an Impact?

NOW Publishing will help you build your book and deliver your message in a powerful, impactful way.

Everyone has a story to tell and NOW Publishing is here to help them bring those stories to life. Whether you have already written a book and need a marketing partner to promote your story, or have an idea for a book that can change lives and inspire others, we are here to help you turn that into something memorable and marketable.

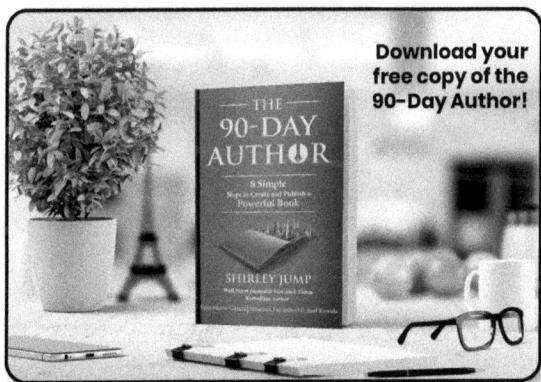

Download your free copy of the 90-Day Author!

EMAIL US!
publish@nowscpress.com

Ask about our
90-Day Idea-to-Author Program!

NOW
PUBLISHING

VISIT US!
www.PublishWithNOW.com

About the Author

For as long as she can remember, Paulee Bowin has been interested in art, writing, and creative arts. A ballet dancer from the age of ten, Paulee has held several unique jobs, including magician's assistant, personal shopper, and leg model. A member of the Professional Association of Visual Artists, as well as a painter, writer, and illustrator, Paulee published her first children's book, *The Girl Who Sings the Alphabet Backwards,* in 2018, which later was chosen as a Book of the Month selection by a Boca Raton magazine. She currently works in the insurance industry and lives with her husband in Florida.

www.ingramcontent.com/pod-product-compliance
Lightning Source LLC
Chambersburg PA
CBHW071711210326
41597CB00017B/2434